IMAGES

At the Beach

Karen Bryant-Mole

Heinemann

First published in Great Britain by Heinemann Library, Halley Court, Jordan Hill, Oxford OX2 8EJ,
a division of Reed Educational & Professional Publishing Ltd.

OXFORD FLORENCE PRAGUE MADRID ATHENS MELBOURNE AUCKLAND KUALA LUMPUR
SINGAPORE TOKYO IBADAN NAIROBI KAMPALA JOHANNESBURG GABORONE
PORTSMOUTH NH (USA) CHICAGO MEXICO CITY SAO PAULO

© BryantMole Books 1998

Designed by Jean Wheeler
Commissioned photography by Zul Mukhida
Produced by Mandarin Offset Ltd
Printed and bound in China

02 01
10 9 8 7 6 5 4 3 2

ISBN 0 431 06316 8

British Library Cataloguing in Publication Data
Bryant-Mole, Karen
At the beach. - (Images)
1.Seashore - Juvenile literature
2.Readers (Primary)
I.Title
574.5'2638

Some of the more difficult words in this book are

Acknowledgements
The Publishers would like to thank the following for permission to reproduce photographs. Bruce Coleman Ltd; 4 (right) and
20 (left) Charles & Sandra Hood, 5 (left) Harald Lange, 17 (right) Janos Jurka, 21 (left) N. Schwirtz, 21 (right) Allan G Potts,
Positive Images; 8 (both), 13 (left), 16 (left), Tony Stone Images; 4 (left) Mike Smith, 12 (left) Lori Adamski Peek, 12 (right)
Claudia Kunin, 16 (right) Darrell Wong, 20 (right) Darryl Torckler, Zefa; 5 (right), 9 (both), 13 (right), 17 (left).

Every effort has been made to contact copyright holders of any material reproduced in this book. Any omissions will be
rectified in subsequent printings if notice is given to the Publisher.

Contents

Animals

There are many different animals living on and around the seashore.

Swimming

Lots of people like swimming in the sea.

Flippers help you to swim quickly.

A mask and snorkel allow you to see and breathe with your head underwater.

Safe sun

It is important to protect yourself from the hot sun at the beach.

Here are some ways to stay safe in the sun.

Shells

You can often find shells on the seashore.

Every shell was once
a home for a sea creature.

Having fun

People like to have fun
on the beach.

12

Which of these things would you like to do?

Full of air

Each of these objects has to be filled with air before it can be used.

Sports

There are lots of sports to try
at the seaside.

sand
yachting

windsurfing

surfing

sailing

17

In the sand

You can use these beach
toys when you play
in the sand.

Have you ever built
a sandcastle?

Plants

Seaweeds are plants that grow in the sea's salty water.

These flowers and grasses are growing in sand.

Souvenirs

People often buy
things to remind
them of their visit
to the seaside.

They are known
as souvenirs.

Glossary

creature animal

mask something that is worn over your eyes
when swimming underwater

protect keep safe

seashore the land around the edge of the sea

snorkel a tube that you can breathe through
underwater

Index